Safety First!

Safety on Your Bicycle

by Lucia Raatma

Consultant:
Michael Taylor
Community Safety Division
National Safety Council

Bridgestone Books
an imprint of Capstone Press
Mankato, Minnesota

Bridgestone Books are published by Capstone Press
818 North Willow Street, Mankato, Minnesota 56001
http://www.capstone-press.com

Library of Congress Cataloging-in-Publication Data
Raatma, Lucia.
    Safety on your bicycle/by Lucia Raatma.
    p. cm.—(Safety first)
    Includes bibliographical references (p. 24) and index.
    Summary: Discusses the safety aspects of riding a bicycle, including such topics as helmets, equipment, traffic rules, hand signals, and visibility.
    ISBN 0-7368-0193-6
    1. Cycling—Safety measures—Juvenile literature. 2. Bicycles—Safety measures—Juvenile literature. [1. Bicycles and bicycling—Safety measures. 2. Safety.] I. Title. II. Series: Raatma, Lucia. Safety first.
GV1055.R33 1999
796.6'028'9—dc21
                                                      98-46239
                                                       CIP
                                                       AC

Editorial Credits
Rebecca Glaser, editor; Steve Christensen, cover designer and illustrator;
    Kimberly Danger, photo researcher

Photo Credits
David F. Clobes, cover, 6, 8, 10, 12, 14, 16, 18
John Lyman, 20
Shaffer Photography/James L. Shaffer, 4

Capstone Press and photographer David F. Clobes wish to thank Scheels All Sports of Mankato, Minnesota, for providing equipment used in the photographs.

Table of Contents

Bicycle Safety

Biking is a good way to go places. Be prepared to ride safely. Check that all your equipment works before you ride. Wear clothes that will not become caught in wheels or pedals. Always wear a helmet.

equipment
the tools used in a sport; biking equipment includes bicycles and helmets.

Helmets

A helmet protects your head if you fall. Make sure you wear a helmet correctly. Your helmet should fit tightly. It should sit flat on your head. The chinstrap should fit closely under your chin.

The Size of Your Bike

Your bike should be the right size for you. A bike that is the wrong size is hard to ride. Your feet should touch the ground when you sit on the seat.

Checking Your Bike

Make sure every part of your bike works before you ride. Ask an adult to help you check your brakes and tires. Your brakes should work well so you can stop easily. Your tires should have enough air. Riding with flat tires will harm the tires.

Being Seen on Your Bike

Drivers need to see bike riders. Wear bright colors when you ride. Make sure your bike has reflectors and lights. Try not to ride at night. But if you do, wear light-colored or reflective clothing. Drivers might not see bike riders wearing dark clothes.

reflective
causing light to bounce off of a surface; reflective tape or clothing allows drivers to see bike riders at night.

Dangers on the Road

Watch out for dangers on the road.
Look for holes and ride around them.
Do not ride fast on gravel. You could
skid and fall. Ride slow down hills.
You can lose control if you ride fast
down hills.

gravel

small, loose stones that
cover dirt paths and roads

15

Intersections

Be careful at all intersections. Stop before you leave a driveway or cross a street. Look left, then right, then left again. Do not cross until the intersection is clear. Walk your bike across busy intersections.

intersection
a place where two or more roads meet; a crossing

17

Traffic Rules

Follow all traffic signs and signals when you ride on streets. Ride with traffic on the right side of roads. This is where drivers expect bike riders to be. Use hand signals to tell people when you will turn.

traffic
the movement of cars, trucks, and buses on roads

Biking on Busy Streets

Always ride single file when you bike with others. Pay attention to traffic on busy streets. Obey signs and stoplights. Listen for horns, sirens, and other sounds. Get off the road if you hear sirens.

Hands On: Learn Hand Signals

Use hand signals when you ride your bike. Hand signals tell others that you plan to change direction or stop. Practice these signals when you bike on a sidewalk or driveway. Then you will know how to use signals when you bike on busy streets.

Left turn

Extend your left arm straight out to the side.

Right turn

Extend your left arm out to the side. Bend your elbow and point your hand upward.

Stopping or slowing down

Extend your left arm out to the side. Bend your elbow and point your hand downward.

Words to Know

chinstrap (CHIN-strap)—a strap that fits closely under the chin and keeps a helmet tight

gravel (GRAV-uhl)—small, loose stones that cover dirt paths and roads

helmet (HEL-mit)—a hard hat that protects the head during sports activities

reflector (ri-FLEK-tur)—a shiny surface that bounces back light

signal (SIG-nuhl)—something that sends a message or a warning

Read More

Boelts, Maribeth. *A Kid's Guide to Staying Safe on Bikes.* The Kids' Library of Personal Safety. New York: PowerKids Press, 1997.

Loewen, Nancy. *Bicycle Safety.* Plymouth, Minn.: Child's World, 1997.

Internet Sites

Florida Children's Safety Center
http://legal.firn.edu/kids/bicycle.html
Illinois State Police Kid's Page—Bike Safety
http://www.state.il.us/ISP/kids/bks000hp.htm
NHTSA's Safety City Bike Tour
http://www.nhtsa.dot.gov/kids/biketour/index.html

Index